Skipton and the Dales

IN OLD PHOTOGRAPHS

Skipton and the Dales

IN OLD PHOTOGRAPHS

Collected by FRIENDS OF THE
CRAVEN MUSEUM

ALAN
SUTTON

Alan Sutton Publishing Limited
Phoenix Mill • Far Thrupp
Stroud • Gloucestershire

First published 1992

British Library Cataloguing
in Publication Data

Friends of the Craven Museum
 Skipton and the Dales in Old Photographs
 I. Title
 942.84

 ISBN 0-7509-0170-5

Typeset in 9/10 Sabon.
Typesetting and origination by
Alan Sutton Publishing Limited.
Printed and bound by
WBC, Bridgend, Mid Glam.

Contents

Introduction

Much has been written about Skipton and the Craven Dales villages. Their pre-Domesday existence and subsequent evolution and development have been extensively researched by professional archaeologists, geologists, historians, naturalists, artists and photographers, and by innumerable amateurs who have been happy to put pen to paper or brush to canvas to describe or illustrate the beauty and character of this unique area. Well known are Dr T.D. Whitaker's *History of the Deanery of Craven*, W.H. Dawson's *History of Skipton*, and Dr Arthur Raistrick's numerous books and papers which have established him as one of the leading authorities on Dales folklore and history. Many novelists, Charles Kingsley and Halliwell Sutcliffe among them, have chosen this beautiful landscape as the background to their romantic novels, and renowned water colour artists Turner and Girtin painted the rugged grandeur of the rocky scenery. In the television era, villages and scenery are extensively used in drama series, and the encouragement of tourism is now the order of the day.

One of the earliest visits to this area is recorded by Daniel Defoe in his journal of 1724, *A Tour through the whole Island of Great Britain*, in which he states that, on leaving Skipton, '. . . we turned south-west which brought us to a place called Settle, a much better town than we expected in such a country. It lies on the road to Lancaster at the foot of the mountains that part the county from Yorkshire upon the River Ribble. Looking forward to the north-west of us we saw nothing but high mountains, which had a terrible aspect and more frightful than any in Monmouthshire or Derbyshire, especially Penyghent Hill. So having no manner or inclination to encounter them merely for the sake of seeing a few villages and a parcel of wild people, we turned sharp north-east.' Some one-hundred-and-fifty years later the appreciation of these wild places had changed; Bailey J. Harker of Grassington and Edmund Bogg were extolling the Dales landscape and history, and outlining the facilities now available – horses, carriages, and accommodation – to would-be explorers.

Airedale, Ribblesdale and Wharfedale, with their numerous tributary dales, have their own individual characters. The mature Aire and Wharfe leave Craven and make their way circuitously to the River Ouse and the North Sea, while the Ribble fails to follow her sister rivers across Yorkshire but as a wayward daughter turns westward into Lancashire. The River Aire is described by John Ogden as a river of 'contrasts and surprises that well repay exploration'. B.J. Harker, in his

Rambles in Wharfedale, 1896, declares, 'to those who live in the din and turmoil of the town or city – there are few places that I would recommend with greater confidence than Wharfedale'. Ribblesdale has unique charm, and of its fells John Ruskin asserted that nowhere else could one experience 'the very heart and meaning of wind'.

The Friends of the Craven Museum have brought together a series of photographs depicting, in some measure, the environment, industry, and leisure activities of the people of the town and Dales. Some are taken from the family albums of members and their friends, having a special significance to them and, it is hoped, capable of arousing a comparable interest in the mind of the readers.

Walter E. Walker
July, 1992

SECTION ONE

Skipton

High Street looking north, 1873. The earliest recorded tenant of the building whose gable end can be seen on the left was Edward Smith in 1707.

High Street with the public library building (left) opened in 1910.

Caroline Square before the building of Woolworths. The man standing in the doorway on the right is probably Tom 'Tinner' Wear. Fattorini's corner is on the left.

Swadford Street with the Ship Hotel on the right. The Ship was entirely rebuilt in 1888. For many years it was the town's main post office.

Keighley Road. Note the sign of the Premier Picture Palace (left), Skipton's first purpose-built cinema, dating from 1913. The tall building on the right was Hargreaves, the dentists. It was demolished in the 1930s to make way for Burtons Buildings.

Sheep Street with Liptons grocers (left). This shop became Breares and then Waterfall Travel. On the right are the steps of the old Town Hall, at the foot of which the uprights of the stocks can still be seen. The stocks were removed in 1840 from their original site in the High Street.

Mill Bridge with Procters, painter, paperhanger, glazier and plumber, *c.* 1910.

The Springs Canal, constructed in 1773 to bring limestone from the Earl of Thanet's quarries to the main Leeds–Liverpool Canal.

Springs Canal and Mill Bridge.

Entrance to Skipton Castle Woods when the sawmill was in operation.

The parish church of the Holy Trinity viewed from Primrose Hill.

Gargrave Road before the building of Park Avenue. On the right is the Roman Catholic school, built in 1854 by the Tempest family of Broughton. Before this date a school for Roman Catholic children had been housed over a shop on the corner of Albert Street and Coach Street. On the left is the Primitive Methodist church, opened in 1878 and demolished in the early 1970s.

Gargrave Road looking towards the town centre, with the turning to Salisbury Street (left). Gargrave Road was constructed in about 1832.

The statue of Sir Matthew Wilson, Skipton's first Member of Parliament, on its original site. In 1921 it was removed to its present position outside the library in order to make way for the War Memorial.

The Ship Hotel, *c.* 1912. A guidebook of 1898 states that it was 'the headquarters for Messrs Thomas Cook & Sons' celebrated "Craven Drives" through the charming valleys of the Aire and the Wharfe – excursions which are much appreciated by the people of the great manufacturing centres of Yorkshire and Lancashire and are becoming more popular every year'.

An eighteenth-century warehouse on the Leeds–Liverpool Canal. The canal reached Skipton in 1773. The loading cover can still be seen on the left and is retained as a feature of the present commercial premises.

Testing Pinder Bridge over the canal with steam rollers, 9 November 1910.

Moor View Swimming Baths in the course of repair. Moor View was opened on 6 April 1907.

Shortbank Road and the baths. The baths were established by Dr Thomas Dodgson, in about 1840, taking advantage of sulphur springs. Writing in 1852, Benson Bailey said that 'Plunge, Shower and Swimming Baths' were available, and also 'Warm and Cold Baths'. There were 'Pleasure Grounds' attached to the baths to which subscribers were admitted free and the public for a small charge. The baths were never a paying proposition and Dr Dodgson is said to have ended his days in the Workhouse. Whatever the truth of this, he is known to have been in reduced circumstances when he died in 1866.

Dyneley House. This was the birthplace of George Geoffrey Robinson who adopted the surname of Dawson and became editor of *The Times*. The house, which was a temperance hotel for many years, has been demolished.

The drawing room at Burnside, the former Independent Methodist Guest House. In 1933 one could stay at Burnside in the height of the season for two guineas (£2.10) per week. Prospective guests were urged to 'Come prepared for a jolly time' and 'Don't forget your music'.

Clay Hall, on the way to Broughton.

Cottages at Mill Bridge. Property at Mill Bridge was purchased for road improvements in 1923. It is likely this photograph was taken at about that time. The site is now a garden.

A 'Whit Sing' in Caroline Square in the 1920s by Sunday School scholars, teachers and supporters. The first Whitsuntide Sunday School celebration in Skipton was held in 1870. At its peak the event attracted about 1,500 people.

The bells of the parish church of the Holy Trinity prior to recasting by Messrs Taylor & Co. of Loughborough in 1921. They were rededicated on 12 August in the same year. Second from right: Mr Randerson (Weights and Measures Inspector).

A stone-laying ceremony at the Baptist Church Sunday School, 4 October 1924. This addition to the school buildings was erected as a memorial to the church members who had lost their lives in the First World War.

Ladies' Victorian weekend at Trinity Wesleyan Methodist church, *c.* 1929. Back row, left to right: Miss E. Davies, Mrs Rimington, Mrs Edmondson, -?-, Miss K. Edmondson. Middle row, left to right: Mrs Clayton, Mrs Pickard, Miss Bailey, Mrs Jackson, -?-, Mrs Lawson, Mrs Stubbs, -?-, -?-. Front row, left to right: -?-, Mrs Daggett, -?-, Mrs Dockeray, Mrs Wilkinson.

Sunday School at the Primitive Methodist Mission, established in the Broughton Road area in 1902. In contrast to the day-school photographs, every child wears headgear of some kind.

The wedding of Charles Walker and Elizabeth Davies, 1905. The group is posed at the rear of the Temperance Hall, now the Plaza Cinema, Sackville Street.

Elizabeth Davies, member of a youth orchestra associated with Water Street Wesleyan Methodist church.

Christ Church School. This school was opened in 1845 and was originally known as the Croft School. There was a proposal to call it Archbishop Benson School after the Archbishop of Canterbury, whose wife was a Sidgwick from Skipton, but nothing came of this.

Trinity Wesleyan Methodist infant school, opened in July 1890.

Christ Church School with Mr Sandland on the right.

In the playground of Christ Church School, *c.* 1938. Left to right: Dorothy Bateman, Iris Whittam, Beryl Turner, John Horner, Victor Burton, Neville Myers, Staverley Timmins, Jean Gill, Dennis Gray.

Reunion of the Brougham Street School May Queens with the headmaster, Arthur Townsend, *c.* 1930. Back row, left to right: E. Bell, -?-, K. Bellamy, E. Mellor, ? Whittingham, E. Clidero, D. Furness, F. Tillotson, E. Potter. Middle row, left to right: ? Tranter, E. Lund, D. Day, A. Townsend, E. Wing, -?-, -?-. Front row, left to right: L. Hargreaves, -?-.

Brougham Street School, *c.* 1923. Back row, left to right: L. Hetherington, ? Hindle, ? Townsend, P. Brookman, ? Greenwood, R. Randall, ? Smith, E. Wilkinson, R. Milner, A. Ryder, R. Barrett, J. Greenwood. Middle row (standing), left to right: E. Townson, A. Thompson, M. Whittingham, M. Simpson, ? Lancaster, -?-, -?-, -?-, M. Cook, W. Walker, I. Macrae. Middle row (sitting), left to right: ? Posket, -?-, O. Horner, -?-, M. Holmes, I. Thomas, M. Fox, D. Bell, E. Mellor, M. Lancaster, -?-, ? Gorton, P. Haigh. Front row, left to right: H. Howcroft, E. Bishop, H. Birtwhistle, A. Windle, F. Lancaster, F. Perkins, H. Hardcastle.

Presentation to F.J.N. Dufty by Sir William Milner of Parceval Hall in the old lecture theatre at the Science and Art School, now Craven College.

F.J.N. Dufty, master at Ermysted's Grammar School and first honorary curator of the Craven Museum.

Prize-winning gala float outside the Primitive Methodist church, Gargrave Road. Skipton Gala was started in 1901 to raise funds for Granville Street Hospital.

Trinity Wesleyan Methodist float on the kind of wet Gala Day to which Skiptonians are only too well accustomed. On the float sheltering from the rain are, left to right: E. Wharton, W. Walker, Mrs Atkinson, ? Chester, R. Rickwood, H. Driver. In the background is Rockville, now occupied by Ackers and Battle.

Seth Marsden (1835–1907), bellman and pinder, outside the Town Hall prior to heading the procession at the Annual Gala.

A commemorative arch across Ship Corner. These arches were erected to mark special occasions at local or national level. Note the old Ship Hotel building on the left.

An outing leaving from the Unicorn Hotel on Keighley Road. The inn was noted for its catering for wagonette parties. It also supplied horses for weddings and funerals.

The Unicorn Hotel, from which this heavily laden coach was about to leave, was demolished for road-widening and was rebuilt in about 1923. The last landlord of the old premises was Mr F. Tunnicliffe.

A charabanc outing leaving from the front of the Town Hall, a recognized starting point for such trips. Part of the canopy which once covered the steps can be seen on the right.

A group outside the Thanets Arms, High Street.

Pierrots from Christ Church school, taking part in the Gala of 1903.

Belle Vue No. 1 football team. The team was associated with the cotton factory of John Dewhurst & Sons Ltd, subsequently part of the English Sewing Cotton Co. Ltd.

Early Skipton football players. Back row, left to right: G.E. Clayton (of Buckden), H.L. Kidd. Middle row, left to right: W.R. Wilkinson, A. Dewhurst, J.B. Dury, W.A. Somervell, W.W. Maude (of Rylstone), G. Bracewell (of Gargrave). Front row, left to right: Cecil Slingsby (noted alpine climber of Carleton), G. Wilson (of Bolton Abbey), Lionel Dewhurst, J.J. Wilkinson.

Skipton Male Voice Choir in the grounds of Ermysted's Grammar School.

'Cow Monday' in the High Street. The livestock market was held in the High Street until 1906.

Preparations for the ox-roasting to mark Queen Victoria's Golden Jubilee, 1887.

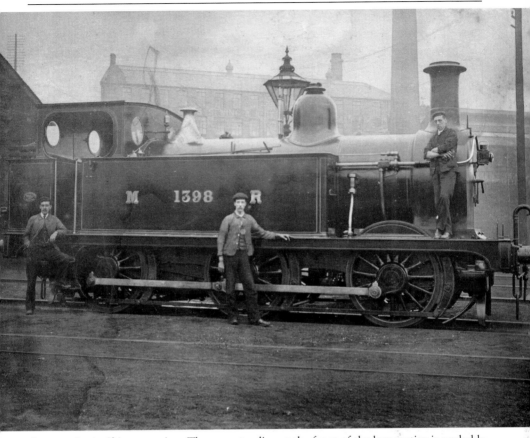

Locomotive in Skipton station. The man standing at the front of the locomotive is probably Albert Wilson from Ducket Street.

The original 'Owd Bill' Motors on Broughton Road. The firm was founded by William Wiseman.

Skipton Castle Woods with a photographer at work in the centre of the picture. In the background is the conduit leading water into Sandy Goit.

Stead's shop in Albert Street.

No. 1 George Street. This is one of ten corner shops on the north side of Sackville Street, three of which were off-licences. The proprietor, John Whalley, his wife, daughter, son-in-law and granddaughters stand in the doorway. John's father Richard was known as 'Yeast' Dick, because the family held the sole agency for the supply of yeast to the retailers and bakers in Skipton and area. The shop was known locally as 'the balm (yeast) shop'.

Skipton Rock Line, laid in the late eighteenth century to carry stone from the quarry to the Springs Canal and thence to the Leeds–Liverpool Canal.

Haw Bank Quarry, in the early twentieth century.

The footpath from Skipton to Embsay, through Haw Bank Quarry, known locally as 'Little Sweitzerland'.

Eastby sanatorium, built for the Bradford Board of Guardians at the beginning of the century. It was later used by Dr Arnott who devoted her life to the successful treatment of tubercular children. The building was put to many other uses, including a brief and disastrous period as a holiday camp.

A milestone on the bridleway over Barden moors. In the background is Lower Barden reservoir.

Skibeden Quarry.

Craven Naturalists' celebration dinner, 1937. Back row, left to right: J. Edmondson, M. Rankin, -?-, A. Jagoe, T.H. Hibbert, T. Nicholson, G. Hurst, F. Midgeley, E. Smith, J. Anderton, A.C. Waterfall, C.C. Cooper, P.P. Illingworth, J. Mitchell. Front row, left to right: E.A. Llewellyn, T.H. Holmes, T.H. Shepley, F.J.N. Dufty, C. Cheetham, A. Mitchell, A. Green.

The wedding of Walter Davies (far left) and Mary Whalley (far right) of Skipton, with Mr and Mrs Whalley (seated). This photograph was taken at the rear of No. 1 George Street.

Skipton Board of Guardians at the Workhouse, 1938. Back row, left to right:
G.B. Harrison, A. Snowden, W.H. Clarke, E.D. Waite, R.G. Procter, J. Bracken,
R. Mosley, J. Demaine, G. Petyt, H.H. Edmonds, D. Slater. Second row, left to right:
T. White, J. Cockshott, T.R. Openshaw, J.W. Gott, R. Hodgson, J. Aldersley,
H. Riddiough, J.H. Preston, W. Hartley, R.R. Wallbank, F. Metcalfe, J.R. Maxfield, Revd
A.E. Chance, T. Breare, E. Townson, R. Edmondson. Third row, left to right:

P. Whittaker, F. Walton, J.S. Windle, H. Hargreaves, G.S. Green, A. Wilson, M.R. Knowles, W.E. Harper, Mrs Somerville (matron), Mr Somerville (master), A. Smith, F.H. Whitaker, H. White, R. Bland, S. Birch. Front row, left to right: W. Duckworth, J. Boothman, Col W.W. Maude, P. Barrett, J. Longstaff, J. Marsh, Mrs Slingsby, J.A. Slingsby, Mrs Spencer, T.F. Hammond, Mrs Hopwood, T. Bellamy, J.S. Hagar, O. Robinson, Lt-Col J.B.G. Tottie, J.D. Brown.

Members of a Skipton choir on an excursion to the Dales. Left to right: -?-, A. Horner, -?-, C. Walker, E. Davies.

Craven Naturalists excursion. Included are: A. Dewhurst, T.H. Holmes, H. Clements, H. Thornton, F.J.N. Dufty, H.C. Rogers, T.H. Hibbert.

SECTION TWO
Airedale

Sutton-in-Craven parish hall stone-laying by J. Bairstow in 1908.

Crosshills Water Company borehole at Crosshills.

Kildwick station on the Midland Railway. The station was opened in 1889 and closed on 22 March 1965.

Leeds–Liverpool Canal at Farnhill.

Airedale Mill on fire, 1906. No trace remains of this mill which was situated between Kildwick and Cononley Lane End.

Cononley station on the Midland Railway. The station opened in about 1889 and closed in 1965. It was later demolished and then re-opened in 1980.

Early motoring days at Gargrave.

Gargrave before the removal of the War Memorial to its present site. The cottages on the left have been demolished.

High Street, Gargrave. Gargrave lies between the Aire and the Leeds–Liverpool Canal. It is the old central parish of Craven and was once a market town.

Fire at Airebank Mill, Gargrave, October 1912. The firm of Johnson & Johnson bought this former cotton mill in 1934.

The Swan Inn, Gargrave. A court for the recovery of small debts was held at The Swan. It was also for a short period the setting for the magistrates court for the Skipton district.

Eshton Hall. Described in 1893 as the 'chief attraction' of the parish of Gargrave, the hall was the home of the Wilson family from 1643. The Wilsons rebuilt the hall twice. In its present form it dates from 1825. The architect was George Webster of Kendal. Miss Richardson Currer built up a notable library here, but it was dispersed on her death in 1861.

Flasby Hall, Gargrave. This is an early nineteenth-century Italianate-style villa which was the home of the Preston family until 1952. During the First World War it housed a girls' school from Scarborough.

Sylvan scene in the closing years of the nineteenth century.

Bell Busk station on the 'little' North Western Railway, later the Midland Railway. The railway was opened in about 1909 and closed in 1959.

The peaceful hamlet of Otterburn. The population was twenty-six in 1801 and reached a peak of sixty in 1931.

Airton Mill. The mill was owned originally by the Dewhurst family. It has seen many changes, including use as a chicken hatchery, and has now been turned into flats. During the Second World War it was used for the manufacture of Dettol.

Kirkby Malham viewed from the church tower, 1951.

Church of St Michael the Archangel, Kirkby Malham. This is a Perpendicular building on the site of an older church.

Church of St Michael the Archangel, Kirkby Malham. Oliver Cromwell is said to have witnessed the wedding here, in 1656, of Martin Knowles of Middle House, Kirkby Malham and Dorothy Hartley of West Marton. Cromwell is supposed to have been on a visit to Calton Hall, the home of Major General John Lambert.

Members of the Craven Naturalists and Scientific Association at Hanlith Hall, Malhamdale, in June 1952. Back row, left to right: W. Holgate, -?-, Miss Brown, Mrs Hudson, Mrs Walker, Mrs Pilkington, -?-, Mr Nicholson, Mr Furness. Middle row, left to right: -?-, -?-, -?-, -?-, Mr G. Hurst, Mrs Fruish, -?-. Front: Mrs Tillotson.

Malham. Note the irregular field-shapes and the drystone walls. Malham Cove can be seen on the left.

Malham from the east.

Malham Beck and bridge. The beck once marked the division between the estates of Fountains Abbey and those of Bolton Priory, which between them owned the entire village.

Gordale bridge on the way to Gordale Scar.

Gordale Scar. This was originally a cave, the roof of which collapsed long ago. One of the most magnificent features of Craven, the cave has been visited and portrayed by many writers and artists, including Wordsworth, Gray and John Piper.

The Buck Inn, Malham, in the early days of motoring. The present building replaces an earlier structure on the same site. It is a good example of the 'estate' architecture favoured by W. Morrison of Tarn House.

Jammy Croft, Malham, *c.* 1935. A break during haymaking. Left to right: William Hudson, Joseph Nelson, Mr Nelson, Hannah Nelson, Margaret Nelson, Walker Foxcroft, Maggie Purcell.

Making rows ('rowing up') during haymaking on King Meadow, King House Farm, Malham, 1960s. The three small crofts in the background were once used during the Malham sheep sales.

Prior Hall Farm, Malham, 1930s. A cart load of hay. Left to right: James Geldard, John Geldard (on the cart), Thomas Henry Geldard. The horse was 'Captain'.

Jammy Croft, Prior Hall Farm, Malham, 1940s. The horse on the left is on the side rake. The horse on the right is standing with an empty hay-cart.

Sheep sale at Malham, *c.* 1885. On the left is the Lister's Arms, on the right the Temperance Hotel. School logbooks record widespread absenteeism in Malham on sale days.

Sheep sale at Malham, *c.* 1900. Each farmer had his own pen in the same place on the green every year and sold his own sheep. This was a development from the earlier system when the small crofts around the village were hired out for the same purpose. At a later date, after about 1915, an auctioneer took over the selling.

Malham Tarn House and Walter Morrison (1836–1921). The Morrison family purchased the Tarn House Estate in 1852 from the Listers. The family was immensely wealthy, having made money in Argentinian ventures and by the manufacture of black crepe. They enlarged and improved the house and laid out the grounds. Walter Morrison was a millionaire philanthropist and Member of Parliament who spent part of every year at Malham Tarn.

Ablutions in Malham Tarn at a training camp for members of the Settle Defence Volunteers, *c.* 1914.

Malham Tarn, covering 153 acres and prized for its fishing since the twelfth century. The tarn waters rest on a bed of impervious Silurian slate, brought near the surface at this point by the North Craven Fault.

SECTION THREE
Wharfedale

The bridge over the Wharfe at Bolton Abbey. There was a bridge at Bolton Abbey as early as 1318. The present structure replaces one that was washed away in a flood on 17 September 1673.

A group of Beamsley almswomen. The hospital, founded in 1593 by Lady Margaret Russell, Countess of Cumberland, consisted of one 'mother' and twelve 'sisters'. It was a circular building with a chapel at the centre and seven rooms radiating out from the chapel.

Beamsley hospital. The hospital was closed in 1985. It was purchased by the Landmark Trust and converted into select country cottages.

The nave of the former priory church at Bolton Abbey. This was used as the parish church after the dissolution of the priory in 1539. The paintings on the reredos were by a local artist, Mr George Bottomley of Crosshills. The tower has been extensively and beautifully restored.

Ruins of the priory of St Mary at Bolton Abbey, a twelfth-century foundation of Augustinian canons. The priory was dissolved in 1539. The last prior, Richard Moone, is said to be referred to in the nursery rhyme 'Hey, diddle, diddle, the cat and the fiddle'.

The Strid at Bolton Abbey. This is a narrow crevice through which the waters of the River Wharfe surge with great violence. Many unfortunate people have been drowned while attempting to jump the Strid. Once in the water there is very little hope of rescue.

Rylstone, the native village of the Norton family. The village was ruined by the Rising of the North in 1569. The pond replaced the village green in the nineteenth century.

The ruins of Barden Tower. This was once a hunting lodge of the Cliffords of Skipton Castle. In 1485 the 'Shepherd' Lord, Henry Clifford, made his home there. The tower was extensively restored by Lady Anne Clifford in the seventeenth century. It was in ruins by the end of the eighteenth century, having been stripped of its roof in around 1775.

The Oak Room at Barden Towers. This room is in the medieval priest's house built by the 'Shepherd' Lord, which later became the farmhouse. It is now in use as a restaurant, and the dresser and plates are still to be seen. The pike on the table is reputed to have been used at Flodden, and the key is the original key of Barden Towers.

Hetton, a small village between Gargrave and Cracoe, with several old houses of interest. The Angel Inn is well known.

Swinden Limestone Quarry. Limestone of a particularly high quality has been quarried here since the end of the nineteenth century.

Two gas-fired kilns at Swinden Quarry.

Linton Old Hall, a late seventeenth-century house with a Georgian extension.

The church of St Michael and All Angels, Linton. This twelfth-century church was rebuilt and enlarged in the fourteenth century and restored in 1861.

The footbridge over the Wharfe at Linton Falls. Known as the 'old tin bridge', it replaced an earlier structure washed away in a great flood at the turn of the century.

Grassington Low Mill and the stepping stones, reputedly the longest set in the country. The mill was originally a corn mill. It was later used for worsted manufacture and, after 1840, for cotton spinning. After a long period of dereliction, the building is now used for housing.

Craven Harriers at the Wilson Arms, Threshfield.

Threshfield with the Old Hall public house on the left.

Threshfield village green. Stocks remain in the centre of the green.

Threshfield Colliery, dating from the seventeenth century. The most recent working was by John Delany, a quarry owner. The colliery was finally abandoned on 4 November 1905.

Rope railway at Skirethornes Quarry, constructed by John Delany.

Rope railway at Skirethornes.

A group at the cutting of the first sod of the Yorkshire Dales Railway, 7 June 1900. Back row, left to right: Edgar O. Ferguson (engineer), J. Lambert (director), John Scott (director), W.A. Procter (director), Walter Morrison (director), Col W.W. Maude (director), W.H. Hutchinson (contractor). Front row, left to right: John Bonny Dewhurst, J.A. Slingsby, Richard Wilson (solicitor).

Grassington station in Threshfield. This station was part of the Yorkshire Dales Railway, Grassington branch.

The first train arriving at Grassington station, 29 July 1902. The attention of the onlookers has been drawn to the man making a speech in an elevated position on the platform.

Threshfield School. The school was founded in 1674 under the terms of the will of the Revd Matthew Hewitt, rector of Linton. The school ceased to be a grammar school in 1875.

Grassington bridge. This is the oldest existing bridge over the Wharfe. It was rebuilt between 1602 and 1609, and then again in 1824.

Alice Wright, secretary of the Friends of the Museum, beside the Wharfe, 1939.

Bridge End, Grassington. This was probably the first modern housing development near the village.

A view of the Wharfe near Grassington bridge.

An Edwardian family enjoying a summer day at Ghaistrills, a picturesque stretch of the Wharfe near Grassington.

John Crowther (1858–1930), 'the Grassington Antiquary' outside his museum. Crowther, who was a chemist by profession, was a noted local historian, botanist and rights-of-way campaigner.

H. Speight pictured at Grassington. Speight was the author of several well-known topographical books on the Dales.

Mr and Mrs Richard Wellock's Golden Wedding, Grassington, 1916.

Mr Boothman, the violinist, of Linton.

The Upper Wharfedale Lads Research Society, visiting archaeological sites in January 1919. This group was started by John Crowther to help him with his antiquarian researches.

The Long Dub, Grassington. This was a long pool in Lower Grass Wood.

A botanical foray in Wharfedale by two members of the Craven Naturalists and Scientific Association, one of whom may be Lister Rotheray. The gift of his book, *Flora of Skipton*, to the Royal Botanical Gardens, Kew, was acknowledged by the director of Kew on 6 September 1900.

Grassington Square, looking towards the Liverpool Warehouse (left of centre). The Liverpool Warehouse was started in 1848 by William Cockshott of Linton Mill as a facility for his workforce and the other inhabitants of Grassington. From about 1860 it was managed by Fieldhouse Holmes and then by his son, Albert. It closed in about 1920 and the premises became the Café Royal.

Grassington Square. The building on the right is Grassington House. It was built in 1760 by Mr Brown, one of the proprietors of the Grassington–Pateley Bridge turnpike road. In the centre is a wagonette used on Dales excursions.

Looking down Main Street, Grassington, after the introduction of a 'bus service'.

Looking up Main Street, Grassington.

Grassington Town Hall (Devonshire Institute), built in 1885 as the mechanics institute. The Primitive Methodist church (right) was built here in about 1908. It was taken down and re-erected in Skipton in 1950.

One of the Grassington 'folds'.

Grassington Square, *c.* 1910. Note the motor vehicle. By this time the village had become a desirable place of residence for Bradfordians.

Grassington, looking down Main Street towards the Devonshire Hotel.

Hardy Grange. This very ancient building was enlarged and improved by the late Mrs Hartley, the owner (1903). She had the surrounding grounds laid out with great care.

Upper Wharfedale volunteers responding to Kitchener's call, 'Your Country Needs You', *c.* 1914.

Kilnsey, with the Anglers Arms on the left.

Kilnsey Crag, a majestic geological feature scoured by a glacier. The flat fields in front of it mark a silted-up lake. It is the site of the Kilnsey Show.

Conistone. This is a village of Anglian origin with a green and lynchett cultivation.

Hawkswick. This is a tiny village with no church, chapel or school. It was described by Ella Pontefract and Marie Hartley in 1938 as 'a pleasantly forgotten place'. In the Middle Ages it was part of the estates of the Percy family of Northumberland.

Arncliffe. This is the largest village in Littondale with a magnificently situated church. Charles Kingsley wrote part of *The Water Babies* while staying here at Bridge End.

Darnbrook Farm. This farm was originally a settlement of the herdsmen of Fountains Abbey. Its roots are in the twelfth century.

Kettlewell, from the tower of St Mary's church.

The Race Horses Hotel, Kettlewell. The inn was built in 1740 and has since been enlarged.

Wesleyan chapel, Kettlewell. Wesleyan Methodism was introduced to the village in 1810 by a minister from Skipton who was pelted with stones as he preached from his gig. The chapel, which was in the former Grassington circuit, is now closed.

A view of Kettlewell. This postcard was sent to Lilian Benson of Bondgate Green, Ripon, in August 1907 from her cousin Esther. Esther, with her baby, Walter, in her arms, is standing outside her mother-in-law's house. A glimpse of 'John's mother' can be seen in the doorway.

The Starbotton postmistress outside the post office.

Starbotton. The name is Norse in origin and means 'the valley where stakes were driven into the ground'. The village had a short period of nationwide fame in 1686 when a flood caused extensive damage to homes and fields. There was countrywide appeal for relief for the sufferers and help was sent from as far away as Cambridge.

The Fox and Hounds, Starbotton. This inn was almost entirely rebuilt in 1834.

Buckden, the last village on the Wharfe. The name means 'the valley of the bucks'. It was the feudal centre of Langstrothdale Chase.

A mail coach with passengers leaving the Buck Inn, Buckden. Tom Airey, of Grassington, and his son operated this service.

The George Inn at Hubberholme. This was the venue for the annual landletting on New Year's Day known as the 'Hubberholme Parliament'.

Hubberholme church is one of the best known churches in Craven. It boasts a rood-screen erected in 1558 during the reign of Queen Mary Tudor. The church escaped the general destruction of such screens in 1571, probably because of the remoteness of the village. The pews are by Thompson of Kilburn, the 'Mouse Man'.

Nether Hesleden, Litton, *c.* 1930.

Litton. The name means 'the village on a torrent'.

Halton Gill, one thousand feet up at the head of Littondale. Trains of packhorses coming up the dale used this hamlet as a halting place on the way to Settle and Hawes.

A cheese-press (centre) in the dairy at Esco House Farm.

Thorpe, 'the hidden village'. This is a tiny hamlet, so well concealed in Wharfedale that it is said to have entirely escaped the Scots raids which plagued Craven in medieval times.

Another view of Thorpe. Thorpe-sub-Montem is the full name. It is noted for honey and, in local legend, for shoemaking.

Elbolton Cave near Thorpe. The Revd Edmund Jones of Embsay (far left) and 'Bishop Bones', a Swedenborgian minister and antiquary, hired contractors (right) to do the 'dig' at Elbolton.

Craven Naturalists and Scientific Association excursion to Elbolton Cave, c. 1887. The group was led by the Revd E. Jones.

Burnsall, looking towards the church of St Wilfred. The village was an early centre of Christianity in the Craven area and there are Anglo-Danish antiquities associated with the church.

Burnsall. Although this village is so far inland, it has an interesting maritime connection: Lord Nelson's paternal grandmother was Mary Bland of Burnsall, who married the Revd Edmund Nelson.

A suspension bridge over the Wharfe, linking Hebden and Burnsall.

Hebden. This was once a centre of lead mining.

The water-wheel at Hebden. This wheel dates from an attempt to exploit the Beever and Cockber lead veins at the end of the nineteenth century. Both veins proved barren. The wheel has gone but the walling of its pit remains at the side of Hebden Beck.

The Metcalfe family and friends at Hebden Hall, *c*. 1903.

Hebden.

Hebden. An earlier view of the same corner of the village.

Hebden. The village school is on the left. The school was built in 1874 to replace an earlier building in use before 1851.

Appletreewick. This was the birthplace of Sir William Craven (1548–1618) who went to London by carrier's cart in about 1561 and rose to become Lord Mayor in 1611. His benefactions in Craven include the restoration of Burnsall church and the founding of a grammar school in Burnsall (which had become an elementary school by 1876).

Skireholme. Thomas Lumb's paper mill after a fire in the 1920s. The cottages were saved because the wind blew the fire away from them.

Skireholme. Fire at the paper mill. The fire broke out at 2.30 p.m. The Keighley Fire Brigade arrived about an hour later and the fire was finally put out around 8 p.m. although some of the rags used in paper making were still smouldering next day.

SECTION FOUR
Ribblesdale

Coniston Cold on the way to Ribblesdale. The name means 'the king's land in an exposed position'.

Hellifield Peel. This house was built in 1441 by the Hammerton family who obtained a licence 'to enclose, crenellate, and furnish with towers and battlements their Manor of Hellifield'. Sir Stephen Hammerton of the Peel was executed in 1536 for taking part in an attempt to reinstate the monks of Sawley Abbey.

Hellifield Peel. The building was occupied as a private house until 1944. It was then, for a time, used as a hostel for displaced persons. It has been dismantled and in ruins since 1954.

Long Preston with the Methodist church in the background. The church was demolished in the early 1970s. On the right is a memorial erected by Thomas Holgate to his father in 1869. The elder Holgate was probably John Holgate, Wesleyan local preacher of Long Preston.

Long Preston, a pleasant village of small greens.

Long Preston station on the Settle and Carlisle section of the former London Midland and Scottish Railway.

Clark's Free School, Wigglesworth. The school was built in 1779 and later became an elementary school. It is now a private house.

Wigglesworth Wesleyan Methodist chapel. The chapel was erected in 1829. It was replaced in 1910 by the present structure, which has been a private house since the 1970s. Note the bicycles on the left.

Robert Mansergh with his delivery vehicle outside Wigglesworth post office and general store, *c.* 1900. These are the original premises onto which Robert added the present shop, which now occupies the site of his provender store on the right.

The hunt outside The Plough, Wigglesworth. Robert Mansergh's blacksmith's shop is in the background, near the tree. It is now a private house.

Main Road, Rathmell. Tom Kelly the postman and Mrs Robinson the postmistress are at the old post office.

Rathmell, College Fold. This was the home of the Revd Richard Frankland (1630–98) which he opened in March 1670 as the first academy in England for the training of dissenting ministers. The academy was held at Rathmell for four years before repressive legislation forced it to move to a number of other locations. In 1689 times were sufficiently settled for Frankland's return to his native village and the academy re-opened at Rathmell for a further nine years.

Quarry House Farm, Rathmell, *c.* 1908. This was farmed by William Whitfield who also kept the village shop. Nellie Whitfield, with her sister Maggie Taylor and daughters Ethel and Clare, stands at the shop door.

Rathmell Schoool, c. 1906. Back row, left to right: Dora Mitton, Alice Simpson, Annie Walker, Robert Mitton, Mark Harrison, Henry Walker, Billy Harrison. Second row, left to right: Mr Hadfield (head teacher), Mollie Geldard, Nellie Simpson, Maude Woods, Marion Walker, Polly Bilsborough, Evelyn Nelson, Mary Jane Taylor, Miss Hayes. Third row, left to right: Sidney Gray, Harold S. Frankland, Norman Nelson, James Simpson, W. Bilsborough, Hilda Harrison. Fourth row, left to right: Lizzie Hall, Alice Bilsborough, Sarah Simpson, Susie Garnett, Thomas Simpson, Rowland Nelson, ? Gray, Arthur Simpson, -?-. Fifth row, left to right: Thomas Nelson, Frank Gray, Ernest Preston, Richard Walker, Elsie Harrison.

Colonel N. Geldard at Rathmell reading room, presenting a souvenir mug to James Taylor to mark the coronation of King George VI, 1937. Mrs L.E. Geldard, the colonel's mother, is sitting in the car. The War Memorial is on the right.

The wedding of W.H. Garnett, joiner, and Martha Harrison, teacher, Rathmell, 1924.
Front row, left to right: Agnes Harrison, Susie Garnett, Eva Harrison, Richard Garnett,
W.H. Garnett, Martha Harrison, Phineas Harrison, Mrs Harrison, Alice Harrison.

Harry Scarborough and James Mansergh mowing rushes on the mill pond at Rathmell sawmill, 1938. The rushes were dried and used as bedding for cattle.

A famer's float built at Rathmell sawmill by the firm of James Mansergh, *c.* 1927. This was probably the last such float made by the firm.

Mill Cottage, Rathmell, a former corn mill, *c*. 1900. Left to right: James Mansergh, Jane Ann Mansergh, Mrs Capstick (Jane's mother).

The timber stores and mill pond at Rathmell sawmill, *c*. 1900. Mrs Mary Mansergh is seated in the centre of the picture. The pond has been filled in and the site is now a housing development.

Langcliffe Methodist church choir visiting Oakleigh, Rathmell, 1934. Back row, far right: George Hallam (choirmaster). Front row, far left: Miss Lilian Burroughs (organist).

Rathmell Methodist Sunday School outing, c. 1938.

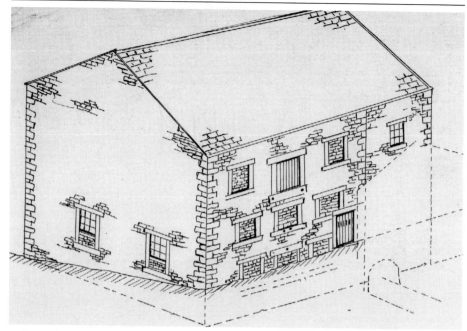

Anley Mill near Settle, now converted to a farm barn. This was a soke mill and then, from 1783, a cotton mill. The original windows (before the fire of 1800) are shown. The mill was very small. The wheel chamber was 27 ft x 9 ft 6 in. As late as 1851 it was referred to as a cotton mill.

Settle, 1834. On the left is the Town Hall, and on the right, with the archway, is the former home of Dr Lettsom (1744–1815), a member of the Society of Friends who spent some years in the town with Dr Abraham Sutcliffe. Lettsom later moved to London and was involved in the movement for free dispensaries for the poor. He also helped to found the Royal Humane Society. The building is now a supermarket.

Duke Street, Settle.

Settle Gala in the 1920s. The League of Nations tableau is passing the shop of
T.D. Smith, grocer, of Lancaster, Settle and Grange.

Settle market place. In the background is the Shambles, a late seventeenth-century open market-hall to which the arches and cottages were added in the late eighteenth century. In 1898 a first floor was added to the cottages and the building assumed its modern form.

The Folly, Settle. This splendid house was built in the 1670s by Richard Preston. His daughter sold it to the Dawson family in 1703 and it has remained in their possession with some intermissions until the present. Known originally as Tanner Hall, it probably acquired its present name in the eighteenth century.

Settle Girls High School, which opened in its present premises in 1913. Henry Longbottom is teaching in the laboratory in July 1959.

The old water-wheel at Brassington Mill, Settle. The wheel, which dates from about 1800, was one of the earliest attempts to make a ventilated wheel.

Giggleswick station.

An ebbing and flowing well at the side of Buckhaw Brow, Giggleswick, 1960. This and the next photograph were taken within five minutes of each other on a winter afternoon.

Ebbing and flowing well. Stories abound of carriers being dismayed by the thought that their horses had apparently drunk a well dry. The earliest known documentary reference to the well dates from 1613.

The Green, Langcliffe. On the right is the Wesleyan Methodist church of 1903 with, adjoining it, the 1852 chapel now converted into a cottage and schoolroom. This is the third Methodist church in the village. It was built on a central site sold to the Wesleyans in 1852 by Mr Bashall who had bought the Langcliffe Mill estate.

Langcliffe. One is not considered a true Langcliffite until one has had at least one soaking in the fountain (left).

Stainforth. This is also known as Stainforth-under-Bargh and Friar Stainforth. It was originally owned by the monks of Sawley Abbey.

Stainforth Foss on the Ribble. One side of the river in Stainforth belonged to Sawley Abbey and the other side to the Tempests of Broughton.

Pen-y-ghent and Studfold from Swarthmoor. At 2,273 ft, Pen-y-ghent is the lowest of the Three Peaks. The name means 'the hill of the winds'.

Helwith Bridge water-driven slate-mill, showing the four saw benches, *c.* 1900.

Horton-in-Ribblesdale sawmill. Note the inclined pipe behind the water-wheel which drove the water turbine which generated electricity for the row of houses. Charlie Read's general store is on the left.

Horton-in-Ribblesdale sawmill. The replacement water-wheel was brought from Helwith Bridge slate-mill when it closed after the Second World War.

Station Road, Horton-in-Ribblesdale, 1920s.

The bridge over Douk Gill Beck, Horton-in-Ribblesdale. This bridge has now been widened. The Three Peaks fell race and a cycle cross race both start in Horton.

Mr Cook in the garden of his cottage on Douk Gill Beck, Horton, 1919.

Griff Hollingshead feeding hens at
Brackenbottom near Horton, August
1919.

Repairing an American 'Oakland' car on the Alum Pot road, 1920.

An 'Aberdonia' car of about 1914. The car was taking members of the Hollingshead family from Horton to Hawes races, April 1919. The car was driven by its owner, Dan Noon of Huddersfield. It had a 20 horsepower engine and body by Park Royal.

Hartley Hollingshead in the 'uniform' of the 'Straddlebugs', knee breeches, Norfolk jacket, long stockings and chrome leather boots. The 'Straddlebugs' were a rambling club which originated in the early 1880s as the Listerhill chapel men's class, Bradford. In winter they encouraged good speakers at their meetings, especially members of the newly formed Independent Labour Party. The alpenstock had been presented to Hartley's father for his sterling services to the club.

Griff Hollingshead on his first ascent of Pen-y-ghent, 1921. Hartley Hollingshead is pushing the pram.

Combs Quarry. This is a notable example of an unconformity with limestone resting on the upturned edges of Horton flags.

The Station Inn, Ribblehead, 1920.

Ribblehead viaduct in the days of steam, *c.* 1950. The longest viaduct on the famous Settle–Carlisle line, it is a triumph of Victorian engineering skill. It was built from limestone quarried between Selside and Ribblehead. The first stone was laid by W. Ashwell on 12 October 1870, and it was completed in 1875. It was originally known as Batty Moss viaduct.

Lodge Hall, Ribblehead. This was the home of the Mason family.

Southerscales Farm. This is thought by some to be a perfect example of a Dales farm. The present house dates from 1725, but there has been a settlement on the site since pre-historic times. The 'scale' element is Norse and means 'a shepherd's hut'.

'Leading' hay by sled, *c.* 1920. John Dowbiggin is with the lead horse, 'Darling', coming down to Southerscales. Griff Hollingshead is on the horse's back. Behind is Tommy, the farm man, with a second sled.

St Leonard's church, Chapel-le-Dale. The original wooden sundial was recently replaced by a metal example.

St Leonard's church, Chapel-le-Dale. The view from the porch looking towards Ingleborough. Over a hundred casualties of the building of the Settle–Carlisle line fill half the graveyard. Many died from illness rather than accidents. The lych-gate is said to have been built so that victims of a smallpox epidemic among the navvies did not have to be taken inside the church.

The Hill Inn, Chapel-le-Dale. The inn is named after Ingleborough and is a popular halting place for motorists and walkers.

Sheep shearing at Dale House Farm, Chapel-le-Dale, *c*. 1914. Note the use of a wooden cratch by the shearer on the right.

A cairn, Whernside, *c.* 1920. Whernside is the highest of the Three Peaks at 2,414 ft.

A thorn tree in Chapel-le-Dale, growing through a rock at the side of the Ingleton–Hawes road.

A cairn, Whernside, in the course of construction.

Cam End, *c.* 1920. The old wooden signpost, which has now disappeared, pointed to Kettlewell and Ingleton. The milestone at the base reads, 'Settle XII miles'. The sign was at a height of 1,432 ft.

Acknowledgements

The Friends of the Craven Museum are grateful for all the help they have received in compiling this book. People have been very generous with their time, their knowledge and their photographs. The following members, friends and institutions have supplied information and pictures:

Miss H. Baines • Mr A. Butterfield • Mrs M. Chadwick • the Craven Museum
the Craven Naturalists and Scientific Association • Mr R. Fell
Mr and Mrs J. Geldard •Mr D. Hannam • Mr G. Hollingshead
Mrs D. Jessop • Mr and Mrs E.H. Longbottom
Mr and Mrs J. Mansergh • Mr P. Mawson • Mr J. Richardson
Mrs R.G. Rowley • Mr J. Skellam • Mr C.S. Smith • Mr and Mrs W. Walker
Mr F.D. Woodall • Mr and Mrs W. Wright.

Our thanks to Valentine Rowley and Peggy Walker for having dealt so efficiently with the typing.